GAQM - CERTIFIED LEAN SIX SIGMA GREEN BELT (CLSSGB) Exam Practice Questions and Dumps

Exam Study Guide for GAQM (CLSSGB) Exam Prep
LATEST VERSION

Presented By: Emerald Books

Copyright © 2020 by Emerald Books

All rights reserved. This book is sold subject to the specification that it shall not, by way of trade or otherwise, be lent, auctioned, hired out, or otherwise distributed without the publisher's prior approval in any method of binding or cover other than that in which it is published, with the exception of in the case of concise quotations exemplified in critical reviews and certain other noncommercial uses legalized by copyright law.

First Copy Printed in 2020

About Emerald Books:

Emerald Books is a publishing house based in Boston, Massachusetts, USA. It a platform that is available both online & locally, it's objective is to provide a community of readers the educational content, literary collection, poetry & many other book genres. Emerald Books is committed to bringing the best of these genres to the consumers. We make it simple for writers & authors to get their books projected, published, advocated, and sell professionally on worldwide scale with eBook + Print circulation. Emerald Books was founded in 2015, and is now distributing books worldwide.

QUESTION 1

Which statement(s) explain an unwanted state when executing SPC?

A. The lower Control Limit for the R chart is equivalent to zero
B. Try to use SPC for tracking transaction times at a warehouse
C. A process is in Statistical Control before execution of SPC
D. The Control Limits are broader than the customer requirement limits

QUESTION 2

If a process has Outliers which pair of charts is best desirable if subgroups will exist for the Continuous Data?

A. Individual—Moving Range
B. Xbar-R Charts
C. Xbar-S Charts
D. nP and P Charts

QUESTION 3

After a Belt has put data through the smoothing process which chart could be used to look for trends in the data?

A. Moving Average Chart
B. Multi-Vari Chart
C. X bar Chart
D. Pareto Chart

QUESTION 4

A Belt determines a Lean Six Sigma project with the conception of a Control Plan. At what point can the Control Plan be closed?

A. Not ever, a Control Plan is a living document
B. Once the Champion signs off
C. Within 30 days of the LSS project review team meeting
D. After the project has been shown at the identification event

QUESTION 5

Multiple Linear Regressions (MLR) is preeminent used when which of these are authorized? (Notice: There are 3 precise answers).

A. Non-linear relationships among the inputs X's and output Y
B. Doubt in the slope of the linear relationship among an X and a Y
C. Relationships among Y (output) and more than one X (Input)
D. Averting the use of a Designed Trial if pointless
E. We suppose that the X's are unrelated of each other

QUESTION 6

Fractional Factorial designs for an trial tactic are used when_____ regarding the multiple metric interaction in a process.

A. Much is identified
B. Little is identified
C. We don't care
D. Data survives

QUESTION 7

A Belt will infrequently do a rapid trial denoted to as an OFAT which stances for_____

A. Just only a Few Are Tested
B. Opposed Factors Affect Method
C. One Factor At a Time
D. Ordinary Fractional Tactic Method

QUESTION 8

Which statement(s) are precise for the Regression Analysis shown here? (Notice: There are 2 precise answers).

A. This Regression is an instance of a Multiple Linear Regression.
B. This Regression is an instance of Cubic Regression.
C. %Cu clarifies the majority of the process variance in heat flux.
D. Thickness clarifies over 80% of the process variance in heat flux.
E. The number of Residuals in this Regression Analysis is 26.

QUESTION 9

The Regression Model for an observed value of Y comprises the term? o which symbolizes the Y axis intercept when X = 0.

A. Correct
B. Incorrect

QUESTION 10

After studying the Capability Analysis shown here choose the statement(s) that are incorrect.

A. The process is correctly assumed to be a Normal process
B. The Mean of the process moving range is 1.78
C. The process is out of Control
D. This Capability Analysis used subgroups
E. Majority of the dimensional values are outside of the tolerance than within

QUESTION 11

The actual trial response data differed rather from what a Belt had anticipated them to be. This is the outcome of which of these?

A. Inefficiency of assesss
B. Residuals
C. Confounded data
D. Gap Analysis

QUESTION 12

Multiple Linear Regressions (MLR) is preeminent used when which of these are authorized? (Notice: There are 3 precise answers).

A. Non-linear relationships among the inputs X's and output Y
B. Doubt in the slope of the linear relationship among an X and a Y
C. Relationships among Y (output) and more than one X (Input)
D. Averting the use of a Designed Trial if pointless
E. We suppose that the X's are unrelated of each other

QUESTION 13

The generation of a Regression Equation is necessary when we_____.
(Notice: There are 4 precise answers).

A. Suppose the relationship to be Linear among the output and inputs
B. Know that there is a non-linear relationship among output and input(s)
C. Need to comprehend how to control a process output by monitoring the input(s)
D. Experience numerous process faults and have no other way to fix them
E. When it is very costly or too late to measure the output

QUESTION 14

The Regression Model for an observed value of Y comprises the term to which symbolizes the Y axis intercept when X = 0.

A. Correct
B. Incorrect

QUESTION 15

Which statement(s) are correct regarding the Fitted Line Plot shown here?
(Notice: There are 2 precise answers).

A. When Reactant rises, the Energy Used rises.
B. The slope of the equation is a positive 130.5.
C. The anticipated output Y is close to -18 when the Reactant level is set to 6.
D. Over 85 % of the variation of the Energy Used is explained by the Reactant via this Linear Regression.

QUESTION 16

Choose all the statements that are correct after studying the Capability Analysis shown here. (Notice: There are 4 precise answers).

A. The process is out of Control.
B. The process is correctly assumed to be a Normal process.
C. The Mean of the process moving range is 1.78.
D. This Capability Analysis used subgroups.
E. Majority of the dimensional values are outside of the tolerance than within.

QUESTION 17

Bias in Sampling is an error because of deficiency of independence amongst casual samples or because of systematic sampling procedures.

A. Correct
B. Incorrect

QUESTION 18

To draw inferences regarding a sample population being studied by modeling designs of data in a way that accounts for casualness and doubt in the observations is identified as_____.

A. Influential Analysis
B. Inferential Statistics
C. Physical Modeling
D. Sequential Inference

QUESTION 19

For a Normal Distribution the Mean, Median and Mode are the same data point.

A. Correct
B. Incorrect

QUESTION 20

When two Inputs have an effect on the Output simultaneously but still appear to have no or little effect on their own this is known as a/an_____.

A. Interaction
B. Oddity
C. Coincidence
D. Impossibility

QUESTION 21

Hypothesis Testing can save time and help evade high costs of trial efforts by using existing data.

A. Correct
B. Incorrect

QUESTION 22

It is a Form II error if we agree to reject the Null Hypothesis when it is in fact correct.

A. Correct
B. Incorrect

QUESTION 23

A Belt experienced an Alpha of .05 and a Beta of .10 and distinguished these are the best general threat levels when running a Statistical test.

A. Correct
B. Incorrect

QUESTION 24

Inferential Statistics is basically regarding Significance. There are both Practical and_____Significance to consider for the duration of an analysis of data in a Lean Six Sigma project.

A. Problematic
B. Impractical
C. Functional
D. Statistical

QUESTION 25

The Central Limit Theorem helps us comprehend the_____we are taking and is the basis for using sampling to assess population parameters.

A. Analysis
B. Kurtosis
C. Threat
D. Route

QUESTION 26

Hypothesis Tests determine the probabilities of alterations among observed data and the hypothesis being solely because of _____ based on the outcome of the P- values.

A. Human error
B. Measurement error
C. Shift alterations
D. Chance

QUESTION 27

The Alpha level of a test (level of significance) symbolizes the yardstick in contradiction of which P-values are measured and the Null Hypothesis is rejected if the P-value is which of these?

A. Not more than the Alpha level.
B. Better than the Alpha level.
C. Better than the Beta and Alpha level.
D. Not more than one minus Alpha.
E. Not more than the power of one minus Beta.

QUESTION 28

A 1-Sample t-test is used when you want to compare the Median of one distribution to a target value.

A. Correct
B. Incorrect

QUESTION 29

When a Belt is examining sample data she have to keep in mind that 95% of Normally Distributed data is within +/- 2 Standard Deviations from the Mean.

A. Correct
B. Incorrect

QUESTION 30

The Mann-Whitney Test is used to test if the Means for two samples are diverse.

A. Correct
B. Incorrect

QUESTION 31

Contingency Tables are used to do which of these functions?

A. Exemplify one-tail proportions
B. Analyze the "what if" situation
C. Contrast the Outliers under the tail
D. Compare more than two sample proportions with each other

QUESTION 32

For the data shown here a Belt questions the three grades are providing the same outcomes. Which statement(s) are correct for proper Hypothesis Testing?

A. The best correct Central Tendency to test is the Means
B. An correct test to test Central Tendency is the Levene's test
C. An correct test to test Central Tendency is the ANOVA test
D. An correct test to test Central Tendency is the Mood's Median test

QUESTION 33

A Six Sigma tool that helps to screen factors by using graphical methods to logically subgroup multiple discrete X's plotted in contradiction of a continuous Y is identified as a
_____Chart.

A. SIPOC
B. Multi-Vari
C. Box Plot
D. Whisker

QUESTION 34

A prime use of using a Multi-Vari Chart is it offers a visual demonstration of two-way interactions.

A. Correct
B. Incorrect

QUESTION 35

Skewed, or Mixed, Distributions happen when data comes from numerous sources that are assumed to be the same but still are not.

A. Correct
B. Incorrect

QUESTION 36

When two Inputs have an effect on the Output together but still appear to have no or little effect on their own this is known as a/an_____.

A. Interaction
B. Oddity
C. Coincidence
D. Impossibility

QUESTION 37

To draw inferences regarding a sample population being studied by modeling designs of data in a way that accounts for casualness and doubt in the observations is identified as _____.

A. Influential Analysis
B. Inferential Statistics
C. Physical Modeling
D. Sequential Inference

QUESTION 38

The flawless sample size is the smallest number of data points needed to provide precisely 6% overlap or threat if one wants a 95% confidence level.

A. Correct
B. Incorrect

QUESTION 39

Bias in Sampling is an error because of deficiency of independence amongst casual samples or because of systematic sampling procedures.

A. Correct
B. Incorrect

QUESTION 40

The Central Limit Theorem helps us comprehend the _____ we are taking and is the basis for using sampling to assess population parameters.

A. Analysis
B. Kurtosis
C. Threat
D. Route

QUESTION 41

Hypothesis Testing can help evade high costs of trial efforts by using existing data.

A. Correct
B. Incorrect

QUESTION 42

Hypothesis Tests determine the probabilities of alterations among observed data and the hypothesis being solely because of chance. This is determined based on the outcome of the_____.

A. Casual acts
B. P-values
C. Standard Deviations
D. R-values

QUESTION 43

It is a Form I error if we reject the Null Hypothesis when it is in fact correct.

A. Correct
B. Incorrect

QUESTION 44

Inferential Statistics is basically regarding Significance. There are both Practical and_____Significance to consider for the duration of an analysis of data in a Lean Six Sigma project.

A. Problematic
B. Impractical
C. Functional
D. Statistical

QUESTION 45

Having an Alpha of .05 and a Beta of .10 are the best general threat levels when running a Statistical test.

A. Correct
B. Incorrect

QUESTION 46

Contingency Tables are used to do which of these? (Notice: There are 2 precise answers).

A. Exemplify one-tail proportions.
B. Compare more than two sample proportions with each other.
C. Contrast the Outliers under the tail.
D. Analyze the "what if" situation.
E. Authorized to data that is Attribute in nature

QUESTION 47

For the data shown here a Belt questions the three grades are providing the same outcomes. Which statement(s) are correct for proper Hypothesis Testing?

A. The best correct Central Tendency to test is the Means
B. An correct test to test Central Tendency is the Levene's test
C. An correct test to test Central Tendency is the ANOVA test
D. An correct test to test Central Tendency is the Mood's Median test

QUESTION 48

The greater the sigma level of a process the better the performance.

A. Correct
B. Incorrect

QUESTION 49

The Six Sigma methodology had its origins at _____ in the late 1980's when William Smith coined the name for quality related work being done there.

A. Motorola
B. Allied Signal
C. General Electric
D. Honeywell

QUESTION 50

Training cost is $4,000 and a project needed an initial investment of $30,000. If the project yields monthly savings of $2,000 beginning after 3 months, what is the payback period in months (before money costs and taxes)?

A. 10
B. 20
C. 27
D. 33

QUESTION 51

Lean Six Sigma's general tactic to solving major challenges related to a process is known as _____.

A. DOE
B. SIPOC
C. DMAIC
D. FMEA

QUESTION 52

Voice of the Customer is a Lean Six Sigma method to determine_____ attributes of a product or service.

A. At least 6
B. The profitable
C. Critical-to-Quality
D. The majority of the

QUESTION 53

Those who are trained to the skill levels of a Black Belt are characteristically utilized to apply Lean Six Sigma methodologies what percentage of their time?

A. 25%
B. 50%
C. 75%
D. 100%

QUESTION 54

A process can be defined as a repetitive and systematic series of steps or activities where inputs are modified or assembled to do a customer desired outcome.

A. Correct
B. Incorrect

QUESTION 55

Customers make a purchase decision based on a number of factors. In Lean Six Sigma we refer to these decision points as CTQ's or as_____

A. Critical-to-quality
B. Conscious thought qualities
C. Conspicuous time quandaries
D. Cost of the quantity

QUESTION 56

Cost of Poor Quality (COPQ) can be classified as Tangible (Visible) Costs and Hidden Costs.

A. Correct
B. Incorrect

QUESTION 57

A worker of ACME Corporation noticed that each loan application that gets accepted is copied four times and is stored in diverse locations in the corporation for no obvious reason. This could be an instance of _____.

A. Internal Failure Costs
B. Appraisal Costs
C. External Failure Costs
D. Prevention Costs

QUESTION 58

The 80:20 rule is related with which of these tools?

A. Pareto Chart
B. Simon's Cross-Functional Tool
C. SIPOC
D. Framing Tool

QUESTION 59

One of the metrics normally used in Lean Six Sigma is DPU. This acronym stances for _____.

A. Deferred planned usage
B. Faults per unit
C. Reduced production utilization
D. Downtime per unit

QUESTION 60

According to the definition of Rolled Throughput Yield which of these items preeminent clarifies the purpose of RTY?

A. A function of Y=f(x)
B. Accounts for losses because of rework and scrap
C. Isolates the increase throughput
D. Determines incremental Growth

QUESTION 61

What is the Cycle Time, in seconds, for a process having a Throughput of 7,200 units per hour?

A. 0.5
B. 2
C. 4
D. 10

QUESTION 62

Which component of waste preeminent clarifies "the cost of an idle resource"?

A. Waiting
B. Motion
C. Inventory
D. Correction

QUESTION 63

The proper functioning of a Visual Factory is dependent upon which of these?
A. Technically trained workers
B. Work space with active 5S
C. Availability of visual tools
D. Breakthrough projects

QUESTION 64

Lean focuses on the sequence of activities and work needed to make a product or a service. This flow is known as a_____.

A. Value-add Flow
B. Production Map
C. Value Stream
D. Operating Procedure

QUESTION 65

Lean Enterprise is based on the principle that wherever work is being done which of these is also happening?

A. Money is being spent
B. Waste is being generated
C. People are producing value added product
D. Waste is being eliminated

QUESTION 66

When constructing a Fishbone Diagram using the _____ tactic is the best classic arrangement.

A. 6M
B. 4M
C. 5M
D. Alphabetical

QUESTION 67

The 5 Why Analysis is just only useful if the probable unrelated variable can be broken down into five probable causes.

A. Correct
B. Incorrect

QUESTION 68

The purpose of a Process Map is to identify the difficulty of the process and to assist in identifying serious steps in the process.

A. Correct
B. Incorrect

QUESTION 69

The very preeminent way to begin an effort to map a process is to do which of these?

A. Interview the process owner
B. Interview the manager of the department
C. Walk the actual process from beginning to end
D. Take snaps of the factory floor at each shift

QUESTION 70

The X-Y Diagram is a tool used to identify/collate potential X's and assess their relative effect on multiple Y's.

A. Correct
B. Incorrect

QUESTION 71

The term FMEA is an abbreviation for Failures Measure Effective Automation.

A. Correct
B. Incorrect

QUESTION 72

When utilizing Statistics, the population is defined as a collection of all the individual data points of interest.

A. Correct
B. Incorrect

QUESTION 73

Which of these is Discrete data?

A. Train arrived at 4:17 pm.
B. Race car used 23 gallons of fuel.
C. Of the 42 people on the bus, 12 went into the station.
D. It took 3 hours and 32 minutes to finish the marathon.

QUESTION 74

Nominal Scale data entails of names, labels or groups and cannot be arranged in any mathematical ordering scheme. Difficult arithmetic functions cannot be effortlessly applied to Nominal Data:

A. Correct
B. Incorrect

QUESTION 75

When looking at a distribution graph, the Mean is defined as the_____.

A. Average based on the sample size
B. Aggression measured
C. Total sample size
D. Measurement based off a quarter of the sample size

QUESTION 76

The difference among the main observation and the smallest observation in the data set is identified as the_____.

A. Breadth
B. Range
C. Spread
D. Median

QUESTION 77

As a form of measurement error, Linearity clarifies a change in accuracy through the expected operating range of the measurement instrument.

A. Correct
B. Incorrect

QUESTION 78

The deviation of the measured value from the actual value is identified as ___

A. Bias
B. Linearity
C. Repeatability
D. Movement

QUESTION 79

The ability to repeat the same measurement obtained with one measurement instrument used numerous times by one appraiser while measuring the identical characteristic on the same part is identified as _____.

A. Repeatability
B. Bias
C. Linearity
D. Reproducibility

QUESTION 80

Process Capability is a function of which of these?

A. Customer requirements
B. Process performance
C. Output over time
D. All of these answers are precise

QUESTION 81

Which of these are precise if Cpk Upper is 2.0 and Cpk Lower is 1.0?
A. The process is not stable.
B. The process is shifted to the left.
C. Cpk must be reported as 1.0.
D. The process Mean is 1.5.

QUESTION 82

A Stable process is a process whose output is consistent over time. A prime tool used to analyze Stability could be a _____.

A. Data Forward Plot
B. Bag Plot
C. Min/Max Plot
D. Time Series Plot

QUESTION 83

Conducting a viable Capability Analysis using Attribute Data one must obtain a fairly large sample set to be statistically sound.

A. Correct
B. Incorrect

QUESTION 84

This output is what form of advanced Capability Analysis?

A. Continuous
B. Binomial
C. Poisson
D. Discreet
E. DPU

QUESTION 85

Fractional Factorial designs for an trial tactic are used when_____ regarding the multiple metric interaction in a process.

A. Much is identified
B. Little is identified
C. We don't care
D. Data survives

QUESTION 86

Some of the tactics used in Lean include station warning lights, tool boards and judoka devices in order that which of these apply?

A. Workers do not utilize individual methods of cleaning
B. Problems are made highly visible
C. Work stoppages are documented correctly
D. Lessen the amount of worker pilferage

QUESTION 87

Instances of a Visual Factory include which of these? (Notice: There are 2 precise answers).

A. White outlines on floor for proper inventory placement
B. Documented procedures with a numerical outline
C. Bad/Good indications of gauge readings with red and green outlines
D. Executing a defect inspection device

QUESTION 88

Standardized work instructions apply to which resource in the process of interest?

A. People
B. Machines
C. Supervision
D. Engineering

QUESTION 89

While management of a corporation must set the stage for all improvement efforts, which of these 5S's is primarily driven by management?
A. Straighten
B. Sort
C. Shine

D. Sustain

QUESTION 90

As part of a Visual Factory plan Kanban cards are created and utilized to identify areas in need of cleaning and organization.

A. Correct
B. Incorrect

QUESTION 91

Kanbans work preeminent with pull systems for determining the timing of which products or services are produced.

A. Correct
B. Incorrect

QUESTION 92

The practice of utilizing Poka-Yoke is also identified as _____.

A. Thorough integration
B. Mistake proofing
C. Onsite inspection
D. Lean controls

QUESTION 93

After a Belt has put data through the smoothing process which chart could be used to look for trends in the data?

A. Moving Average Chart
B. Multi-Vari Chart
C. X bar Chart
D. Pareto Chart

QUESTION 94

A Belt determines a Lean Six Sigma project with the conception of a Control Plan. At what point can the Control Plan be closed?

A. Not ever, a Control Plan is a living document
B. Once the Champion signs off
C. Within 30 days of the LSS project review team meeting
D. After the project has been shown at the identification event

QUESTION 95

In the late 1980's William Smith coined the name Six Sigma for a methodology that had its origins at_____ for quality related work being done there.

A. Honeywell
B. Allied Signal
C. General Electric
D. Motorola

QUESTION 96

Training cost $6,500 and a project needed an initial investment of $47,500. If the project yields monthly savings of $3,500 beginning after 4 months, what is the payback period in months, before money costs and taxes?

A. 9.7
B. 15.4
C. 19.4
D. 23.7

QUESTION 97

The acronym for the defined tactic taken by Lean Six Sigma to solve major challenges related to a process is which of these?

A. DOE
B. DMAIC
C. SIPOC
D. FMEA

QUESTION 98

Voice of the Customer is a Lean Six Sigma method to determine _____ attributes of a product or service.

A. At least 6
B. The profitable
C. Critical-to-Quality
D. The majority of the

QUESTION 99

A process can be defined as a repetitive and systematic series of steps or activities where inputs are modified or assembled to do a _____ outcome.

A. Revenue total
B. Month end
C. Customer desired
D. Budgeted

QUESTION 100

Customers make a purchase decision based on a number of factors. In Lean Six Sigma we refer to these decision points as CTQ's which stances for_____-.

A. Cost of the quantity
B. Conscious thought qualities
C. Conspicuous time quandaries
D. Critical-to-quality

QUESTION 101

Cost of Poor Quality (COPQ) can be classified as either Tangible (Visible) Costs or Hidden Costs.

A. Correct
B. Incorrect

QUESTION 102

The Purchase Orders for Glenn Manufacturing Corporation were being copied by a worker and sent to four diverse departments but still just only one department took an action based on the information in the PO. This is an instance of_____

A. External Failure Costs
B. Appraisal Costs
C. Internal Failure Costs
D. Prevention Costs

QUESTION 103

According to the definition of Rolled Throughput Yield which of the resulting items preeminent explain the purpose of RTY?

A. A function of Y=f(x)
B. Determines incremental Growth
C. Isolates the increase throughput
D. Accounts for rejects and reworks

QUESTION 104

One of the metrics normally used in Lean Six Sigma is DPU. This acronym stances for _____.

A. Deferred planned usage
B. Faults per unit
C. Reduced production utilization
D. Downtime per unit

QUESTION 105

The 80:20 rule is related with which of these tools?

A. Pareto Chart
B. Simon's Cross-Functional Tool
C. SIPOC
D. Framing Tool

QUESTION 106

What is the Cycle Time, in minutes, for a process having a Throughput of 360 units per hour?

A. 0.167
B. 0.333
C. 0.667
D. 1.333

QUESTION 107

The proper functioning of a Visual Factory is dependent upon which of these?

A. Technically trained workers
B. Work space with active 5S
C. Availability of visual tools
D. Breakthrough projects

QUESTION 108

Use of the _____ tactic is the best classic arrangement when constructing a Fishbone Diagram.

A. Chronological
B. 6M
C. 5M
D. Alphabetical

QUESTION 109

When creating a Cause and Effect Diagram the team needs to continually broaden their view as well as drill down until they identify all the potential _____ Effecting their process.

A. Line operators
B. Root Causes
C. Inventory issues
D. Customer requests

QUESTION 110

The very preeminent way to begin an effort to map a process is to do which of these?

A. Interview the process owner
B. Interview the manager of the department
C. Walk the actual process from beginning to end
D. Take snaps of the factory floor at each shift

QUESTION 111

The X-Y Diagram is a tool used to identify/collate potential X's and assess their relative effect on multiple Y's.

A. Correct
B. Incorrect

QUESTION 112

With the use of Statistics we define the population to be a large enough sample set of data such that you can analyze it and draw conclusions as to all of the data.

A. Correct
B. Incorrect

QUESTION 113

Which of these is discrete data?

A. Train arrived at 4:17 pm.
B. Race car used 23 gallons of fuel.
C. Of the 42 people on the bus, 12 went into the station.
D. It took 3 hours and 32 minutes to finish the marathon.

QUESTION 114

When looking at a distribution graph, the Mean is defined as the_____.

A. Average based on the sample size
B. Aggression measured
C. Total sample size
D. Measurement based off a quarter of the sample size

QUESTION 115

The_____is important for the reason that it offers an assess of the probability of an event happening depending on the Standard Deviation from the Mean.

A. Shewhart Principle
B. Pareto Rule
C. Mean/Mode Spread
D. Empirical Rule

ANSWERS

1. Correct Answer: D

2. Correct Answer: B

3. Correct Answer: A

4. Correct Answer: A

5. Correct Answer: CDE

6. Correct Answer: B

7. Correct Answer: C

8. Correct Answer: AD

9. Correct Answer: A

10. Correct Answer: A

11. Correct Answer: B

12. Correct Answer: CDE

13. Correct Answer: ACDE

14. Correct Answer: A

15. Correct Answer: CD

16. Correct Answer: BCDE

17. Correct Answer: A

18. Correct Answer: B

19. Correct Answer: A

20. Correct Answer: A

21. Correct Answer: A

22. Correct Answer: B

23. Correct Answer: A

24. Correct Answer: D

25. Correct Answer: C

26. Correct Answer: D

27. Correct Answer: A

28. Correct Answer: B

29. Correct Answer: A

30. Correct Answer: B

31. Correct Answer: D

32. Correct Answer: D

33. Correct Answer: B

34. Correct Answer: A

35. Correct Answer: A

36. Correct Answer: A

37. Correct Answer: B

38. Correct Answer: B

39. Correct Answer: A

40. Correct Answer: C

41. Correct Answer: A

42. Correct Answer: B

43. Correct Answer: A

44. Correct Answer: D

45. Correct Answer: A

46. Correct Answer: BE

47. Correct Answer: D

48. Correct Answer: A

49. Correct Answer: A

50. Correct Answer: B

51. Correct Answer: C

52. Correct Answer: C

53. Correct Answer: D

54. Correct Answer: A

55. Correct Answer: A

56. Correct Answer: A

57. Correct Answer: A

58. Correct Answer: A

59. Correct Answer: B

60. Correct Answer: B

61. Correct Answer: A

62. Correct Answer: A

63. Correct Answer: C

64. Correct Answer: C

65. Correct Answer: B

66. Correct Answer: A

67. Correct Answer: B

68. Correct Answer: A

69. Correct Answer: C

70. Correct Answer: A

71. Correct Answer: B

72. Correct Answer: A

73. Correct Answer: C

74. Correct Answer: A

75. Correct Answer: A

76. Correct Answer: B

77. Correct Answer: A

78. Correct Answer: A

79. Correct Answer: A

80. Correct Answer: D

81. Correct Answer: C

82. Correct Answer: D

83. Correct Answer: A

84. Correct Answer: B

85. Correct Answer: B

86. Correct Answer: B

87. Correct Answer: AC

88. Correct Answer: A

89. Correct Answer: D

90. Correct Answer: B

91. Correct Answer: A

92. Correct Answer: B

93. Correct Answer: A

94. Correct Answer: A

95. Correct Answer: D

96. Correct Answer: C

97. Correct Answer: B

98. Correct Answer: C

99. Correct Answer: C

100. Correct Answer: D

101. Correct Answer: A

102. Correct Answer: C

103. Correct Answer: D

104. Correct Answer: B

105. Correct Answer: A

106. Correct Answer: A

107. Correct Answer: C

108. Correct Answer: B

109. Correct Answer: B

110. Correct Answer: C

111. Correct Answer: A

112. Correct Answer: B

113. Correct Answer: C

114. Correct Answer: A

115. Correct Answer: D

www.ingramcontent.com/pod-product-compliance
Lightning Source LLC
Chambersburg PA
CBHW070900220526
45466CB00005B/2064